A STEP-BY-STEP BOOK

BUDGERIGARS

GEORG A. RADTKE

Photography: Dr. Herbert R. Axelrod; H. Bielfeld; Gary Doeslex; Michael Gilroy; Ray Hanson; Fred Harris; A. Jesse; Burkhard Kahl; Harry Lacey; H. Reinhard; Vince Serbin; Norma Veitch; Wayne Wallace. Humorous drawings by Andrew Prendimano.

Originally published in German by Frankh'sche Verlagshandlung, W. Keller & Co., Stuttgart under the title *Unser Wellensittich*. First edition © copyright 1986 by Franckh'sche Verlagshandlung, W. Keller & Co.
©Copyright 1988 by T.F.H. Publications, Inc. for English translation. A considerable amount of new material has been added to the literal German-English translation, including but not limited to additional photographs. Copyright is also claimed for this new material.

© **1988 by T.F.H. Publications, Inc.**

Distributed in the UNITED STATES by T.F.H. Publications, Inc., One T.F.H. Plaza, Neptune City, NJ 07753; in CANADA to the Pet Trade by H & L Pet Supplies Inc., 27 Kingston Crescent, Kitchener, Ontario N2B 2T6; Rolf C. Hagen Ltd., 3225 Sartelon Street, Montreal 382 Quebec; in CANADA to the Book Trade by Macmillan of Canada (A Division of Canada Publishing Corporation), 164 Commander Boulevard, Agincourt, Ontario M1S 3C7; in ENGLAND by T.F.H. Publications Limited, Cliveden House/Priors Way/Bray, Maidenhead, Berkshire SL6 2HP, England; in AUSTRALIA AND THE SOUTH PACIFIC by T.F.H. (Australia) Pty. Ltd., Box 149, Brookvale 2100 N.S.W., Australia; in NEW ZEALAND by Ross Haines & Son, Ltd., 18 Monmouth Street, Grey Lynn, Auckland 2, New Zealand; in SINGAPORE AND MALAYSIA by MPH Distributors (S) Pte., Ltd., 601 Sims Drive, #03/07/21, Singapore 1438; in the PHILIPPINES by Bio-Research, 5 Lippay Street, San Lorenzo Village, Makati Rizal; in SOUTH AFRICA by Multipet Pty. Ltd., 30 Turners Avenue, Durban 4001. Published by T.F.H. Publications, Inc. Manufactured in the United States of America by T.F.H. Publications, Inc.

Contents

INTRODUCTION

As no other bird, the budgerigar has won the hearts of people all over the world. Yet it was discovered only 150 years ago and has been bred in captivity for the past 130 years.

Besides being comparatively easy to keep and propogate, there are also many other reasons for the ever increasing popularity of this smallest of parrots: above all, their confiding temperament, the close attachment of the singly kept budgie to humans, and not least their amazing talent for mimicking the human voice and all sorts of other sounds puts them at "number one on the charts" of cage birds.

This book is addressed to all those who derive joy from house pets as a replacement for the rapidly disappearing natural world. It is hoped that it will impart in an easy to understand, clear, and fun to read manner everything you need to know about the budgerigar in order to understand these birds, provide them with appropriate accommodations, care for them properly, make them hand-tame, teach them to talk, and prevent illnesses. I would be pleased if I have succeeded in this purpose.

FACING PAGE:
The domestic or common budgerigar with green-yellow plumage is originally from Australia. The first budgerigars arrived in England in 1840 and soon captivated European bird fanciers, exported by the thousands to supply the demand for the "unusual" and "exotic" bird. The budgie is known scientifically as *Melopsittacus undulatus*.

Because today almost all pet shops offer budgerigars in many colors at affordable prices throughout the whole year, it is no problem to purchase such a bird. Nevertheless, the purchase should be thoroughly considered and prepared for well beforehand, because

BUDGERIGAR PURCHASE

the acquisition of a house pet on a whim or because of the persistent requests of children has been regretted by many who have not considered what is involved. One should first carefully read the following "checklist" before the purchase and answer the questions honestly and unemotionally.

Where will I keep the bird?

The cage should be as large as possible, and must absolutely be large enough for the bird to spread its wings fully.

The location must be free of drafts and have plenty of sunlight. If possible, no smoking or cooking should be done in the room, nor should the light be left on for half the night.

Will I be able to offer the bird liberty regularly?

Among the principal dangers that budgerigars are exposed to when kept at liberty are poorly closed windows and doors, windowpanes without drapes, poisonous house plants, and incompletely covered aquaria or stock pots.

FACING PAGE:
In addition to the basic green-yellow budgerigar,
an array of other colors and plumage patterns are
available today. This beautiful blue and gray
budgie is the result of a planned breeding of
ancestors with known genetic characteristics.

One may have to curb the urge to acquire too many budgies if one does not have the space and the time to care for large numbers of birds.

Can I and do I want to find the time that is necessary for the appropriate keeping and care of a budgerigar?

To good keeping and care belong not only regularly feeding, cleaning of the cage, and liberty, but also daily attention—above all with singly kept birds. And we should not forget: a budgerigar can live for 12 to 14 years.

Single bird, pair, or flock?

Whether to choose a single bird, a pair, or a flock depends in part on the personal preferences of the bird fancier, the available time, and the available space.

Budgerigars are by nature social birds which generally live in fairly large flocks and do everything together. One should, therefore, only keep a single bird if one can find the necessary time during the day to give the bird attention and to talk to it. A singly kept bird that must stay alone in a house without people for a fairly long time will eventually die of sadness.

To be sure, the budgie is able to adjust its habits if its owners must work all day, in that it sleeps a lot during the day and then becomes all the more active in the evening—then, however, one must find the time for it. For this reason, I would sooner advise the acquisition of a pair or even a small flock of budgies for people whose job places great demands on their time.

If one keeps a pair, then the two birds will occupy themselves with each other the whole day and will not especially miss the absence of people; rather they consider them more as welcome food dispensers. And when one has more time, it gives great pleasure to watch everything the two birds do. With some patience, one can also get two budgies although this is somewhat more difficult than with a singly kept bird.

The fear of unwanted offspring is usually unfounded with a budgerigar pair, because a pair kept alone seldom—if at all—breeds. Budgerigars are by nature colony breeders; a single pair is thus lacking the stimulus, the competition, one might say, provided by other pairs. In order to guard against any eventuality, however, one can also keep two birds of the same sex together—whereby males are more compatible than females. Females are more likely to quarrel, although this is also a part of the normal life of a bird. Serious injuries never occur as long as no male is added as a third. If one wishes to keep more than two budgerigars together, then one should separate them strictly by sex if fighting and offspring are not wanted.

Budgies are gregarious birds, occupied most of the time with one another. When kept too long in isolation a budgerigar can die with no apparent signs of physical illness.

Unless indisposed or too old, budgies display an alert look that makes them such appealing pets. Those that are trained to talk inevitably become priceless companions.

Apart from developing less of an attachment to people, the disadvantages of keeping several birds are more noise, because a lively flock of budgerigars is not always quiet, and the increased time that must be spent on care, although fairly large modern cages are equipped with high bottom drawers or isolating panes of glass. Likewise, there are automatic feeders and drinkers in various sizes that can be hung in the cage, which permit even several birds to be left alone for a few days.

Is anybody in my environment allergic?

Unfortunately, house pets must often be given up, given away, or sold time and again, because someone in the family turns out to be allergic to feathers or hair. When possible, shouldn't this be tested before the acquisition of a house pet?

Budgerigar—yes!

If we have answered all of the questions favorably then nothing else actually stands in the way of the purchase. If we are now standing in the pet shop, or at a breeder's in front of a flight cage with its flock of varicolored budgerigars, choosing can be difficult, and new questions arise:

Which color should I choose?

When you get right down to it, all plumage colors are beautiful; it is all in the eye of the beholder.

Yellow and white budgerigars with red eyes (they lack the dark pigment in the eyes, so that the blood shows through) are somewhat more sensitive to light, and therefore show a tendency to flutter in panic briefly if exposed to a sudden change from darkness to light. They calm down again, however, as soon as their eyes have become adjusted to the change.

In addition, light plumage is somewhat more susceptible to soiling than is dark plumage.

A good example of the variety of colors and plumage patterns in budgerigars.

Is the selected bird healthy?

We should always take our time when purchasing a bird and should guard against being led astray by love at first sight. Above all, the budgie should be healthy and lively.

The seemingly especially tame ones, which make no attempt to avoid a finger and possibly allow themselves to be stroked, are unfortunately not always what they seem, because very few are already tame. It is more likely a sort of apathy, which indicates illness or at least indisposition.

It is best to take a step back and observe the birds undisturbed. We should never buy birds that fluff up their plumage, that perch quietly in a corner, or even tuck their heads in their plumage. If at all possible, one should also avoid buying birds with one or more of the following symptoms:

– The plumage is untidy and dull, and is often even soiled or stuck together around the vent area.
– The eyes are dull, closed, or stuck together.
– The nostrils are caked or gummed up with deposits or a slimy liquid is flowing out.
– The bill is broken off, ripped, scaly, or swollen like a sponge.
– The breathing is irregular or rapid.
– The toes are deformed or some are missing.
– The droppings in the cage are pasty, watery, or slimy.
– The bird perches impassively, sticks its head in its plumage as if to sleep, but rests on both legs instead of one, as healthy birds do.

Youngster or adult?

If we want a budgerigar that is supposed to become hand-tame and a good talker, then the budgie should, if possible, still be nest young at the time of purchase; that is, not much older than four to six weeks. The younger the bird, the more quickly it will become tame and the more closely attached it will become to its human mate.

Of course, very few pet shops or breeders are able to offer nest young budgerigars all year round, because the breeding birds also need rest, and very few breeders have so many pairs that they can breed at least some of their birds throughout the year. It is thus possible that one could have to wait for a while, but in return will obtain a very young bird taken right from its parents. The first days in the new home are critical for such a young bird, because the separation from the parents and siblings combined with the change in environment are a considerable upheaval in his life. One must therefore watch the bird very carefully in the first few days, and above all make sure that

Using the tail length as an indicator of age, you can easily recognize the youngest individual in this row of budgies.

it is eating. Without food intake the bird will die within two days, because birds this young have a very rapid metabolism.

Once the first hurdle has been cleared, however, the little budgie will consider people as a replacement for parents and siblings within a few days, and the spell will be broken: one will have an attached budgerigar that is imprinted on humans. This is all fine and good, but also carries a lot of responsibility, because a tame bird of this kind will no longer be able to associate with other birds and will pine if left alone from more than half a day.

But it is by no means a tragedy if the newly acquired budgerigar is already three or four months old. Most budgerigars can still be tamed up to an age of about six months, although the older they are, the longer it takes. On the other hand, they are not as difficult to acclimate.

How do I recognize a youngster?

A very young, only just independent budgerigar has a shorter tail than an adult and completely dark eyes (black or red) without a light iris ring surrounding the interior of the eye.

The light iris ring usually does not become distinct until the fifth to sixth month. All color varieties with dark, so-called normal wavy markings also have a clearly recognizable juvenile plumage. The wavy pattern extends over the lighter forehead up to the base of the nostrils.

The ground colors in green and blue are duller, less intense, and the throat spots, which are round and usually stand out clearly in adults, are either only suggested or are apparent only as indistinct hatching. With the completely light budgerigars, such as the yellows, whites, and light pieds, these markings of course are not present, but even they exhibit the completely dark eyes.

One can also recognize young budgerigars by the differently colored cere (the area above the beak in which the nostrils are found) in comparison to adults: young males have a uniform bluish-pink cere, and adult males (with the exception of a few color varieties) have a bright blue cere. Young females have a bluish-white cere and a whitish border is always present on the inside of the nostrils. Adult females exhibit a dark-brown or chalk-white cere.

One of the famous exceptions to the rule are the recessives or Harlequin pieds (dark spots scattered over a yellow or white background, with a green or blue belly). They do not develop a light iris ring even with increasing age; their eyes remain a uniform dark color for life. The males do not develop a blue cere; it remains pink their whole lives as in the youngsters. The same is true of the closely related completely yellow or white budgies with black eyes, but not of those with pink eyes. In these birds the age can be determined only by the iris ring. The gradual change in coloration, brought about by the molt in the adult plumage, begins in the third to fourth month and is completed by the eighth to ninth month. At first a few light feathers appear on the forehead, until finally it is completely yellow or white. The new feathers on the breast and rump are a more intense green or blue, the first round throat spots appear, and the new flight and tail feathers are longer. Budgerigars in this transitional stage are not particularly attractive, but the condition is temporary, and as long as the juvenile molt has not been completed, such birds also soon become acclimated to

Identificatiion of the sexes by means of the color of the cere may prove difficult for a person without previous experience in observing a stock of budgerigars.

a new environment and can still become tame.

In general, more and more dealers are buying from breeders who belong to associations. These breeders mark their birds with closed bands that can only be put on in the first days of life and cannot be removed. In addition to the serial number, the year of birth is always stamped on such bands, so that no deception can occur, at least with the age. It is advisable to ask for such budgies, even if they are somewhat more expensive.

Male or female?

In general, female budgerigars do not learn to talk as well as males. On the other hand, they are less impetuous, want to fly less, and learn tricks more easily. When annoyed, some females have a tendency to nip a little harder.

Some practice is needed for accurately distinguishing between the sexes, however, and mistakes are occasionally made. Above all, one must have the opportunity to closely examine and compare a number of birds. As we have already learned with distinguishing between youngsters and adults, the color of the cere gives a fundamental indication of the budgerigar's sex.

The New Home

Before the budgerigar (or budgerigars) arrives, the new home should already be prepared and the cage should be in its final location. Continued rearranging, perhaps in the hope of finding better location, is—particularly during the acclimatization period—much resented by the bird.

HOUSING

Which is the right cage?

Budgerigar cages are available in various sizes, colors, and shapes and in quite different price ranges—depending on taste and pocketbook. Roomy cages, which are longer than high, with horizontal bars, a plastic basin—for the sake of easier cleaning—and a door that can be securely closed (to the side or upward) and cannot act as a guillotine, have proved to be the most practical.

Nevertheless, the cage must meet three basic conditions:
1. It must be large enough that its occupant can stretch and can also fly a short distance in it.
2. The bars must run crosswise, because budgerigars like to climb and can climb well, and this is hard to do with vertical bars.
3. It must be easy to clean.

Cages in which the top also opens upward, so that climbing provisions and playing apparatus fold outward and are

FACING PAGE:
If you wish to provide your pet budgie with a
perch from a natural plant, be sure that the plant
is non-poisonous and free from insecticides.

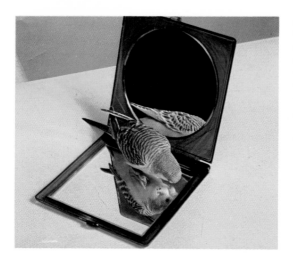

A solitary budgie will be kept entertained by any object that is reflective, like a mirror. Be sure the mirrors you provide do not have sharp edges that can cut the legs or the face of your pet.

easily accessible to birds kept at liberty are very practical. Such a cage will quickly become an assembling point for birds kept at liberty, because they can easily enter for food and water and their favorite toys are easy to reach. For the provider, the advantage of such cages is that the birds do not soil their environment as much, because when they are playing in their favorite place, droppings and lost feathers fall to the bottom of the cage.

Because the budgerigar has a well-known penchant for gnawing, cages with metal bars are the best suited. With today's brass-coated cages one no longer has to be concerned with verdigris, because the material has been treated to prevent it.

In the past, round cages, in which the birds were supposed to develop so-called staggers, were always warned against. Today, round cages are no longer as greatly feared, because they are now provided with horizontal instead of vertical bars, and most budgerigars no longer have to spend the whole day in the cage, but are allowed to leave it for at least part of the day.

There are also cages with a removable pane of glass over the entire front. They allow the bird to be seen clearly—as long as the glass is always clean! Besides more frequent clean-

ing, the principal disadvantage of these cages is the lack of direct contact with the bird, which is particularly important during the acclimatization period.

When keeping more than two budgerigars, one requires a flight cage or a small aviary. Such cages are also available in the most diverse styles and price ranges. With these cages it is particularly important that they are easy to clean. The larger flight cages for two or more budgerigars have, depending on size, one or two easy to remove drawers for cleaning and, depending on the price range, a double bottom, so that when cleaning the cage no mess lands on the floor when the drawer is removed.

Furnishing the cage

The new bird home should not be too crowded with interior furnishings, so that the bird can still move freely.

All cages are mass-produced with matching, more or less suitable food and water bowls. The standard bowls are readily replaceable and are usually equipped with a protective cover so that they cannot be as easily soiled from above. This is a great advantage, but most budgies that are acquired from breeders are not accustomed to something of this sort. In their breeding boxes and aviaries, breeders usually use only open

An array of store-bought articles for a budgie; a swing, ladder, and bell. These articles can all be cleaned with water and soap, and gnawed parts smoothed by a wood file.

containers or automatic feeders and drinkers. For this reason, newly acquired birds, as a rule, are not adjusted to a covering and in the beginning have difficulty in finding food and water. Nest-young budgerigars, in particular, often starve—to the great disappointment of their owners, who cannot explain the sudden death of their new pet. For this reason, one should always spread some food on the floor of the cage during the first few days at home and hang some spray millet in the cage. If the birds do not find the water right away, this is not as serious, because budgerigars can survive for days without water, and seldom drink outside of the breeding season. (Nevertheless, fresh water should of course always be available!)

In addition to these standard food and water bowls for a budgerigar cage, there are also a number of others on the market, which one simply inserts between the bars of the cage at the height of the perches, or sets up or hangs in the cage.

If one must leave the bird alone over the weekend and there is no vacation substitute to feed the bird, then one should always use an automatic feeder and an automatic drinker. These automatic devices can be filled with fairly large quantities of food and water, and they have the further advantage that the food and water cannot become soiled. The bird must, however have the opportunity to become adjusted to these automatic devices beforehand, to feed and drink from them, and, before leaving the bird alone, one must test to make sure that the water and food can run through freely.

A food receptacle placed away from the cage's floor has the advantage of keeping the seeds free from excreta and urine.

A portable bath designed for a budgie's cage. It is also possible to use it as a food or water tray.

A bathing facility, as is used for canaries and their relatives, is not an absolute necessity for budgerigars, for budgies in the wild seldom bathe, and some do not bathe at all. They clean their plumage with the aid of their bills and a substance from the preen gland on their rumps, and prefer a rain shower or rubbing in wet leaves. If one wants, one can acclimate one's Budgie to the use of a bathing facility by putting a few lettuce leaves in the water, in which the bird can then roll. After the bath, the leaves must be removed, because wet or even rotting lettuce can be damaging to the bird's health.

Toys—a must for single birds that are often left alone for long periods of time—are available in the most diverse models. The small plastic balls and bells should, if possible, be hung in the cage on a completely smooth string or very small chain. Many a budgerigar has been hung up by the banded leg on fibrous strings or large-linked chains and has died a very painful death if help was not immediately available, or at the very least has dislocated a leg or suffered a compound fracture (which heals only with difficulty, if at all).

Mirrors are also very well liked, even though experience is mixed here: the mirror makes the budgie think that another of its kind is present, which is very comforting for the bird, particularly in the first weeks after being separated from its parents and siblings. But if the sex drive awakens later, then in the attempt to feed the other member of its species, the mirror will become smeared with regurgitated food and will also be used for other purposes that may not be to everyone's taste. For this reason, one should only place a budgie mirror in the cage temporarily.

Swings are also very well liked and serve as the preferred roosting place for many budgerigars after a while.

A Natural Diet

Wild budgerigars of the Australian plains primarily feed on various grass seeds, which they eat in all stages of development. Accordingly, the most important basic food for our birds is a mixture of various seeds.

Basically: seeds

FEEDING

Budgerigar mixtures are sold prepackaged by a number of companies in pet shops. Most of the brands are good, as long as the products are not too old. The older the seed mixtures are, the more of their nutritional value they lose, and food that has gotten too old (packaged longer than 12 months previously)—once so good—can lead to malnutrition.

Prepared seed mixtures contain various kinds of millet, either in equal proportions or a larger percentage of one sort or another, depending on the wholesale supply. This does not matter, as long as the product is fresh, clean, and above all capable of germination, although the birds, in part individually, in part fundamentally, prefer certain kinds over others. Always readily eaten are, for example, white millet; the pale yellow La Plata panicum millet, which consists of small, oval seeds; the even smaller, dull yellow Senegal millet; and the gray, and therefore less attractive, Japanese millet.

On the other hand, the most attractive kinds like the gold-colored Moroccan millet and the red Dakota millet, both consisting of large, round seeds, are usually not as well liked

FACING PAGE:
A color variety of budgie called lutino. To some extent the yellow color can be intensified by a diet that is rich in carotene. Carrots, for example have an abundance of this pigment.

A combination of dried fruit and seeds is also available commercially. Even a bird needs a different menu at times.

because of the greater hardness of the shells. For the sake of a more attractive appearance (to the owner; the bird doesn't care about such things) most manufacturers insist on mixing in these kinds. If one mixes one's own food in the pet shop from open goods—which is possible in some shops—one can easily leave out these two kinds. A good mixture should contain, at the very least, 15 percent canary seed (these are the elongated,

Compacted seeds in a stick (illustrated here) or in a cake form usually are composed of a variety of bird seeds. A budgie often first picks his favorite kinds and may leave other types untouched.

Vitamins in liquid form can be mixed with the dry food or mixed with the drinking water. Budgies in their prime may not need vitamin supplements critically, but older budgies need them in order to stay in relatively good health.

pointed seeds in the food), or, better yet, double that, or 30 percent. Unfortunately, canary seed is often missing from many mixtures, even though it is one of the few foodstuffs that has become less expensive in recent years.

Almost every budgerigar mixture also contains two to five percent hulled oats–nutritious and therefore good. But a greater percentage should not be fed, because cage birds, in particular, otherwise easily become obese.

Two heaping teaspoons of this seed mixture, the basic food, per bird per day are completely sufficient, although food intake differs from bird to bird, and according to studies by Muller-Bierl, varies from one to 19 grams per day (the lower limit seems to me to be too low and the upper limit too high).

In general, budgerigars do not readily overeat, so that filling a normal food bowl about three-quarters full is about right for a single bird. With proper feeding, a few whole seeds will be found in the food bowl the next day after blowing away the empty hulls.

Blowing away the empty hulls is very important and should be done twice a day with young budgies, because these birds husk seeds so that the empty hulls mostly fall back into the food bowl, so that the bowl soon contains quite a thick layer of empty hulls on the surface. Young, inexperienced budgerigars have starved because they either could not find the food underneath or because the inexperienced bird keeper thought that the bowl was still completely full!

Older budgerigars, on the other hand, throw the hulls out of the food bowl with a few vigorous strokes of their bills

Natural millet, being nutritionally rich, should not be considered as a staple food to be given regularly. Offer millet as an additive for enriching the regular diet occasionally.

in order to get to the food underneath, and if they do not find any, they will soon draw attention to the fact by loud scolding. But one should never allow it to get this far, because budgies have a very rapid metabolism. Even a few hours without food, with the exception of the nighttime hours spent at rest, can greatly weaken a budgerigar and make it susceptible to illnesses.

A supplementary feeding of half-ripe ears of native grasses and grains is exceptionally valuable—and has the added benefit of saving food (and money). A bunch hung in the cage will keep the bird busy for hours. In the months of June and July, oats and wheat are the easiest to find. But, as was already mentioned, only feed them in moderation. Grass seeds can be found starting in June and continuing into the fall. With grass seeds one must experiment to find out what the birds like best. The only important thing is to make sure that the grass panicles and heads are fresh and are only collected in clean sites that have not been treated with chemicals.

Another kind of seed that should be mentioned is spray millet, which is available—although it is not exactly cheap—on the market in ripe sprays from four to 12 inches (ten to 30 centimeters) long. This food is preferred over all others by virtually all seed eaters, and is also very well tolerated by even very young, sick, or old birds. Spray millet should, however, only be fed in moderation—as a treat, a reward, as rearing food, or as a food for sick birds. Too much spray millet quickly leads to obesity. With a nest-young budgerigar, the sprays that are hung in the cage should only be replaced when they have been

26

completely eaten. From an age of five months on, the birds should be given at most one spray a week.

Seeds can be offered in a dry, soaked, or sprouted state, but dry seeds should always be available and soaked or sprouted seeds should be offered when no other green food is available. In the sprouted seed, a transformation of fat, protein, and starch into more basic substances and an increase in vitamin B takes place.

Soaked seeds are prepared by rinsing the desired amount of seed well in lukewarm water, then barely covering it with lukewarm water in a dish for 12 to 24 hours, and finally allowing the seed to swell in a warm place. Before feeding, the soaked seed should be allowed to drain thoroughly in a sieve and should then be dried slightly in a towel. Uneaten swollen seed must be removed from the cage in the evening. It becomes sour or moldy over time, and is then not at all suitable as a food for our budgerigar.

In the wild budgerigars eat both dry food (seeds) and green food (grass, foliage, fruit, etc.). So, to make the diet of budgies in captivity complete, they should be provided with fresh green food, too.

As social birds, budgies prefer to feed together. Unlike solitary birds, a budgie will not drive another away from the seed tray.

To sprout seed, one pours the seeds in one layer in a large dish or the saucer of a flowerpot and lets it stand in a warm place for about 24 hours covered with lukewarm water. Then the water is poured off, the seeds are thoroughly rinsed in a sieve under running water, drained, and finally put back in the dish—this time covered with a pane of glass—and allowed to stand in a warm place for another 24 hours. After this time, the proper stage for feeding has been reached if one can see tiny white radicles on the greatly swollen seeds. When feeding sprouted seed, the uneaten remains must also be removed from the cage. The food bowls for the sprouted seeds must be thoroughly cleaned with a brush and hot water before the next filling.

For convenience, dehydrated green food can be given when it is not possible to offer fresh greens.

Sprouting seeds in the home requires very little effort. Simply scatter bird seeds on a layer of soil, moisten with water, and then put away in a warm place. Be sure the place chosen is beyond the reach of other seed-eating animals, like rodents.

Green sprouted seed cultures are just as easy to prepare, in that one sows some millet and canary seed in a good potting soil in boxes or flowerpots, and places the containers in a warm, humid location (in summer, a balcony is a good place). The green seedlings are fed when they have grown about one to one-and-one half inches (two to three centimeters) out of the ground.

A bird does not live by maize alone

A budgerigar fed year after year only with seeds, possibly only dry ones, is no different than a person who eats only potatoes and bread—although these are basic foodstuffs. The supplementary feeding of green and succulent foods is very important for budgerigars, especially since in the wild they eat dry seeds only during the few months of year they are fully ripe. The rest of the year they eat the plant parts in all stages of growth and maturity. Supplementary food should be as varied as possible, but always fresh and unsprayed.

Lettuce is always most welcome. Depending on the time of year, we can offer leaf and head lettuce and endive, but always only in small amounts. Too much green food, particularly if it is quite damp, easily leads to indigestion. The lettuce must always be thoroughly washed and dried; wilted remains should be removed as quickly as possible.

Further variety is provided by pieces of carrot and cucumber, a piece of sweet apple or juicy pear, or a piece of fig. Berries are not readily eaten, and most oranges are too sour.

Budgerigars are very conservative when it comes to eating. They generally will not touch unfamiliar foods at first.

It certainly does not hurt if one has to remove untouched wilted food until budgie finally tries some. And even should it take two weeks or more, one day he will take a taste and will then expect such treats.

This also applies to fresh tree branches for gnawing, which many budgerigars are afraid of when they are put in the cage for the first time. For people who live in the middle of the city, pieces of tree bark for gnawing can be substituted for fresh branches. It is possible that a fruit grower will be happy to give you some pruned branches in the spring.

Even if dry seed is ignored when such supplements are given, it still must always be sufficiently available to prevent diarrhea, all the more so if the budgerigars are not yet acclimated to succulent foods.

An array of fresh food that a budgie accepts. Any of these foods that cause digestive upsets in a budgie should not be given again, or can be offered only in very limited amounts over an extended period of time.

Feeding

Cuttlefish bone serves as the principal source of minerals for many bird species. It is inexpensive and is usually provided with a metal clip or fastener.

Just as essential: minerals

A calcium block, which is marketed by various companies as a budgerigar mineral block, is also critical for maintaining the bird's health. Young birds, in particular, require a great deal of calcium for bone formation, and older birds also need calcium regularly for molting.

Whether these blocks are green, white, or pink is not so important; their consistency and what they are made of are what matters. Good calcium blocks should contain, besides calcium, various minerals that a budgie also requires, and they should neither be too hard nor too soft. Blocks that are too hard are not readily eaten; ones that are too soft are sometimes crumbled to pieces within a few hours as a diversion, whereby the remains on the bottom of the cage become soiled and lose their value. A side effect in the use of the calcium block is bill wiping. The bill of a cage bird, if it lacks natural use, may grow excessively long and then must be clipped regularly.

All seed eaters require small stones that serve as grindstones in their crop for processing seeds. These small stones are themselves ground down over time and therefore must constantly be replaced. For this reason, budgerigars must have coarse-grained sand available at all times. Because all birds require a great deal of calcium and other minerals for bone and feather formation, a special bird grit has been developed, which consists of finely ground shells and other natural mineral components. Shell grit is already present in good bird sand. Whoever uses a different kind of sand can buy clean, not too coarse shell grit in the pet shop and mix it with the sand or add more to prepackaged bird sand.

31

It all comes down to proper care

To the proper care of one or more budgerigars belong:

- Appropriate accommodations.
- Natural diet.
- Keeping the cage and its furnishings, particularly the food and water bowls, clean.
- Bill and claw care.
- Care of the plumage.
- Preventive measures against illnesses.

CARE

Budgerigars should have a light, well-ventilated location and, if possible, should get their share of sunlight. This of course does not mean that the cage should be unprotected and drafty or should even be placed in the full glare of the sun. In any case, the bird must be protected against draft. In a light, sunny location, the bird should also be able to move to a shaded place in the cage.

The birds do not make any particular demands regarding the temperature of the environment, but drastic changes in temperature must be avoided. Room temperatures between 65 to 68 degrees F (18 and 20 degrees C) are the most suitable for keeping budgerigars—in winter as well. At these temperatures the plumage is also much sleeker and more colorful than at higher temperatures.

If a small flock of budgerigars is kept in an indoor aviary, it is better to install it in a cooler entranceway than in an overheated room. Breeders maintain a temperature of only 10 to 14 degrees C in winter in their breeding facilities, and have very good success. Nevertheless, if one must heat one's house to 21 degrees C and above for reasons of health, one need have no fear that the budgerigar will suffer because of it. One must, however, expect to put up with untidy plumage and more frequent molting.

Cleanliness—the first commandment

The cleaner the bird's environment, the better it will

TROPICAL FISH HOBBYIST

Helping marine, freshwater, and reptile hobbyists for 42 years

• January 1994 •
$2.95/$3.95
Canada $3.95/£2.30

The Tiniest Danio
Colorful Plants

ISSN 0041-3259

Let *Tropical Fish Hobbyist* magazine show you how to enjoy the tropical fish hobby to the fullest. Open up a whole new fascinating world with your own personal subscription to the largest, oldest and most colorful aquarium and tropical fish magazine.

YES! Please enter my subscription to *Tropical Fish Hobbyist*. I enclose payment for the length I've selected. U.S. funds only.

- ☐ 1 year—$30.00
  12 BIG ISSUES
- ☐ 2 years—$55.00
  24 ISSUES
- ☐ 3 years —$75.00
  36 ISSUES
- ☐ 5 years—$120.00
  60 ISSUES

Canada, add $11.00 per year; Foreign add $16.00 per year. Please allow 4-6 weeks for your subscription to start.

Prices subject to change without notice.

☐ SAMPLE ISSUE—$3.50 ☐ LIFETIME MEMBERSHIP $495.00 (maximum 30 years)

☐ GIFT SUBSCRIPTION. Please send a card announcing this gift. I would like the card to read:

_____

SEND TO:

Name _____

Street _____ Apt. No. _____

City _____ State _____ Zip _____

CHARGE my: ☐ VISA ☐ MASTER CHARGE ☐ PAYMENT ENCLOSED

|_|_|_|_|_|_|_|_|_|_|_|_|_|_|_|_| (Minimum order charge $15)

Card Number

Cardholder's Name (if different from "Send to:")

_____

Cardholder's Address (if different from "Send to:")

_____

_____
Cardholder's Signature

TEAR ALONG PERFORATION AND ENCLOSE WITH PAYMENT

Budgies preen not only their own plumage but also that of other budgies as well.

feel. Food and water containers should be washed out daily with hot water before they are refilled. The cage must be cleaned at regular intervals. When keeping a single bird, it will usually be enough if one thoroughly cleans the base (that is, the plastic basin) once a week with hot water and a brush and then spreads fresh sand on the bottom.

With a pair or flock, this procedure will have to be performed more often because of the greater accumulation of dirt. The sand in the drawers of fairly large indoor aviaries will not necessarily have to be replaced every week. In these aviaries it

Unsightly conditions resulting from infection caused by parasites such as mites, can be controlled with the proper medication. However, a thorough cleaning and disinfection of a mite-infested cage or aviary is a must in order to stop an infestation.

Sanded perch covers not only protect a wood perch from gnawing but also provide a rough surface that wears away the claws and beaks. Once soiled and worn out, they can be replaced easily. There is no more need to remove and clean the perch itself.

is sufficient to rake the floor weekly to bring the lower layers of sand to the top and to replace all of the sand only once a month.

Once a month one should also perform a general cleaning, that is, in addition to the bottom of the cage, also thoroughly clean the bars and all interior furnishings with a brush and hot water.

Modern cages are easy to remove from their bases and are correspondingly easy to clean. If the budgies are not yet confiding and therefore cannot be kept at liberty in the room during the cleaning, they will—with careful handling—stay on the upper perches while the wire top of the cage is removed and placed on a layer of newspaper.

The perches and in all likelihood the swing as well, should be brushed off under hot water as needed; usually this will already be necessary after two days. Wilted greens and fruit must always be removed from the cage by evening.

Bill and claw care

To bill and claw care belongs the need for enough rough climbing provisions, on which the claws can be worn away, and for twigs, branches, and mineral blocks for gnawing.

Excessively long claws are usually easy to recognize, but usually go unnoticed until the bird starts frequently fluttering its wings because it has snagged its claws somewhere.

Correct way of holding a budgie when trimming overgrown claws. Be sure there is a good source of light strong enough to shine through the claw.

Older budgerigars occasionally exhibit a tendency for excessive claw growth despite natural branches and mineral blocks, and sometimes their upper mandible grows over the lower mandible almost down to the neck. The excess horn of both the bill and claws must then be cut back to a normal size, otherwise the bird will be greatly hindered in climbing and feeding.

To clip the claws, one holds the bird belly down in the left hand. The head should lie between the middle and index fingers; the other fingers hold the foot so the toes can be seen clearly and unobstructedly. The toes with the claws must now be held up to a light source, because only with back lighting will the blood vessels that run through the claw be clearly visible. These blood vessels should never be cut; they bleed quite heavily and, of course, cause the bird pain.

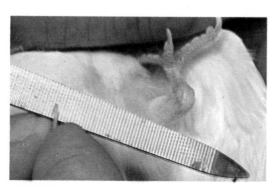

An ordinary nail file will smooth out ragged or too pointed claws.

The overly long claw is cut a few millimeters above the blood vessel, always following the curved direction of growth of the nail—never perpendicular to it—with sharp nail scissors or clippers. With proper handling the bird feels just as little during this procedure as we do when we clip our nails, even if it struggles—which it only does because it does not like to be held on its belly.

Anyone who does not feel capable of performing this procedure can go to the veterinarian for nail clipping.

As a rule, the clipping of the toe nails or bill is only necessary with older budgies, starting in about the fourth to fifth year of life. There are some exceptions to this, in particular with birds that in youth already exhibited a slight, and therefore at first virtually undetectable, bill deformity. The cause is usually an inadvertent injury to the still soft, tiny bill in the first days of life by the parents when feeding or through pressure during the brooding of large-headed young. For this reason, one should also carefully examine the bill when purchasing a bird.

The clipping of the bill is best left to the veterinarian or an experienced breeder or bird keeper.

Plumage care

Daily liberty, keeping in not too warm and not too dry rooms, and an occasional shower belong to plumage care and to the bird's general well-being. Budgerigars, which come from arid regions, are not accustomed to bathing in water puddles, but are well aware of the refreshing effect of a rain shower or bathing in damp leaves. The majority of captive budgerigars also prefer rolling in damp lettuce leaves and being sprayed with a plant mister to taking a bath in a bathing facility. There is also another almost natural method of bathing that will provide the tame budgie much pleasure. It must, however, become acclimated to this method: we carry the hand-tame bird on the back of the hand into the bathroom or kitchen and leave it perched on the hand under the slightly running faucet over the sink. At first, we only allow the faucet to drip and can then tell from the bird's reaction whether it likes it or not.

If it flies away immediately, then it is either not dis-

Quickly dry a wet budgie with a towel after a bath, especially on a cold day. Budgies catch colds when chilled, too.

posed to bathing or was initially frightened by the unexpected drops of water. We try again the next day, until it understands what is going on—which will soon be the case with most budgies.

If, on the other hand, it starts to groom its plumage right with the first drops, then it is adjusted to bathing, and we can turn the water on a little higher. The bird will enjoy it and will completely soak its plumage by fluffing and shaking, and then clean and smooth it with its bill. Now the faucet should be turned off.

One or two baths a week using this method does the budgerigar a lot of good and contributes a great deal to a sleek, glossy plumage. With molting birds, such baths help the bird to complete molting more quickly.

If possible, bathing should be done before noon, so that the bird has time for its plumage to dry completely. The water must not be too cold, but also not too warm. Budgies like lukewarm water best; water that is too warm is unpleasant to them and can just as easily lead to colds as water that is too cold.

Once he is brought into his new home and has been carefully placed in the prepared cage, one should first leave the new acquisition completely undisturbed and keep the enraptured children away from him until he has become acclimated to his new environment. This can take hours, and sometimes even days, because these small birds differ individually just as much as people do.

ACCLIMATING

Some perch unhappily at first, at any rate completely quietly, but observe their environment more carefully than we can imagine, and become wild as soon as a person they don't know yet approaches them. Others climb apparently cheerfully and untiringly around the cage, at the same time stand on their heads and do somersaults, or creep on their bellies over the bottom of the cage and try to stick their heads in each corner, as if they wanted to play hide-and-seek. They are, however, far from cheerful and do not in the least feel like playing. Behavioral biologists describe these actions as displacement behavior, which is a behavior pattern that commonly occurs in all animals in conflict situations. With these seemingly pointless gymnastic exercises, the bird is trying to divert both itself and its observer from the feelings of fear that are controlling it. Man and bird must go through this time for better or worse.

FACING PAGE:
A fully trained budgie that is already acclimated
will not panic but perch quietly anywhere, such
as on the top of the cage or on the body parts of
its owner or handler.

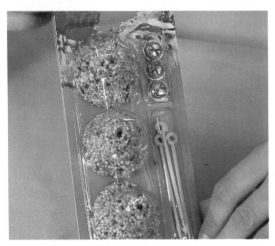

This package of bird seeds compacted in the shape of a bell also includes holders and small bells. Even the most timid budgie will be tempted to eat the seeds and play with the bells.

Once the budgie begins to pick at his first seeds, the first hurdle has usually been cleared. If the bird then goes back to the perch afterwards, as a rule the highest, and makes eating sounds (whetting of the upper against the lower mandible that calls to mind chewing of cud by cattle, and may have a similar function), the future keeper can approach the bird cautiously with deliberate movements. If the bird remains perched, which will be the case most of the time, then one cautiously brings one's face close to and talks pleasantly to the bird. What one says at this time makes no difference and is not yet part of the talking instruction, because the bird is still much too upset to learn. Rather, the first positive reaction of a young budgerigar to this approach is a sort of winking, as if the bird is acknowledging the person's presence. This should not of course be anthropomorphized, because in the bird's language it has a different meaning. It means something like: I do not have to be afraid of the big creature, its voice reassures me. From this time on the bird will scarcely continue to flutter in panic when one approaches the cage.

Several budgerigars are treated in the same way. They will react with the eye winking less, but, on the other hand, will not be as frightened from the start, because, after all, they are not alone, and, as we all know, there is strength in numbers.

In no event may we let the budgerigars out of the cage in the first few days. They would rush around wildly, fly into walls and windows, and would have to be caught with the aid of a carefully used net—hardly a good method for taming them! The cage door must stay closed for the first eight days. They must first become thoroughly at home in their cage; they must also have time to observe and become familiar with their environment from inside. For this reason it is also important to always keep the cage in the same place. Just as important is the accustomed food, of which we therefore bring a small supply from the pet shop or breeder. We can always change to a different mixture later, but a change in environment and food at the same time could endanger the budgie's health. We should also buy some spray millet. Spray millet is, to be sure, too expensive and not healthy to use as a permanent food, but during the acclimatization period, and for nest-young budgerigars in particular, it is a strengthening food and treat all in one. We should hang the sprays in the cage in such a way that they can be reached by the bird from the topmost perch. Even the most timid budgie baby will not be able to resist the attraction for long, and the first step to taming has been made.

Children in the household should be encouraged to talk, but not to yell or scream, to a pet budgie. Experience shows that budgies can get frightened by any loud voice.

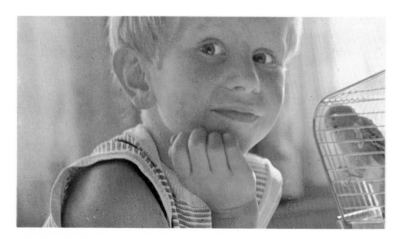

The first step to hand-taming can take place inside the cage. Avoid sudden movements that can cause a budgie to flee and possibly injure itself upon striking the walls of the cage.

How will my budgie become hand-tame?

The three commandments for taming a newly acquired budgerigar are:

1. No hectic movements.
2. Stop the taming attempts when the bird becomes restless.
3. Patience, patience, and more patience.

One should already start getting the bird used to the hand in the first days in the cage. This is particularly important for the single bird, which, after all, is supposed to become finger-tame within a short time. We move the hand with the back facing upward cautiously through the door of the cage and approach the perching bird from the front. If he initially retreats, perhaps to the floor of the cage, then we interrupt the procedure until he has calmed down again. Then we begin anew and attempt to softly press the curve of the hand against his belly. One must have patience at this stage, because it won't always succeed at the first try, but little by little it will, because the pressure that pushes him backwards will force him to climb on the hand so as not to lose his balance. If he then perches steadily on the hand, then we have already succeeded. We let him perch for a while, even if the toenails, with which the little bird at first holds tight in fear, do not exactly produce a pleasant sensation on the skin! We talk to the bird reassuringly all the while, and finally maneuver him carefully back on the perch. If he jumps off instead, this is not too serious. From this time on he will scarcely be afraid of the hand, and soon we can also carefully scratch his head with a finger. All budgerigars like this very much, because they also do it mutually with their bills in the wild. Birds that live communally engage in social grooming of this kind. With budgerigars kept singly in captivity, the human finger replaces the social partner. The bird quickly becomes acclimated to it, and soon he will press against the bars when you approach, so he can be scratched with the finger from outside the cage. At the same time, the head will be held at an angle or bowed, and the feathers will be raised in the place he wants scratched.

The bird should be hand-tame after, at most, eight to ten days. It will generally go somewhat more quickly with younger birds; older ones will need more time. Before familiarity with the hand has been achieved, however, the birds should not be let out of the cage.

In a fairly large family, all family members, if possible, should become familiar with the bird, except for small children, who do not yet have a sense for it; older children can be given guidance. Children who love animals often do this with a great deal of cleverness and patience; the higher voices of women and children are pleasant to the budgerigar's ear, because they are similar to their own. Men with deep voices are more likely suspect.

The acclimatization to other house pets is a subject in itself. For this an especially large amount of patience and sympathetic understanding are needed, and one should not be misled by the photographs in some magazines showing a cat with a budgerigar perched on its head. After all, a bird is first of all a prey animal for all cats. Everything else is a matter of acclimatization, but even then both animals should not be left alone with each other for long! With a dog, jealousy must be contended with, because at first everything centers around the new arrival, and the dog is no longer the accustomed center of attention. But this jealousy will pass with reasonably constant treatment, and the pictures of a dog and bird eating from one dish are for the most part not faked.

The first liberty

When the big day for the first liberty in the room has arrived, one must first carefully make sure that:
1. Doors and windows are closed.
2. Drapes are drawn.
3. Heaters are out of reach or well screened.
4. No open water containers are standing around.
5. The wall sockets are well-covered and no poisonous plants are within reach.

To begin the first liberty one carefully puts—as usual—the hand in the cage. When the bird is steadily perched on it, one slowly draws the hand with the bird from the cage. Rarely will the bird immediately take off in the unfamiliar environment of the open room. First of all, he will remain on the familiar hand or run up the arm to the shoulder in order to feel more secure at a higher point. From here he then begins to fly in small circles, always returning to the familiar person. Even if he particularly likes to fly back to the head as the highest point at first, which on account of the hairdo or bald spot is not to everyone's taste, one has succeeded if the bird comes back on his own.

Later, one can carefully disaccustom the budgie from this landing place by holding out the hand for him after every head landing. If acclimation to the hand was carried out properly, then he will climb onto it on his own, perch like a falcon, and will allow himself to be carried back to the cage on the hand—which is most useful if the liberty must be cut short for reasons of time.

Should the budgie happen to become frightened by something and immediately take off from the hand into the room, he will fly to one of the highest points after a few rounds, not infrequently a curtain rod, and at first will make no attempt to fly from there. We must absolutely never chase after him with a broom or a similar implement; this would only wipe out everything that has been accomplished for a long time to come. It is much better to let him have his way and in the meantime attend to our usual pursuits, because he will certainly become hungry eventually. What then? We simply hold up the familiar hand with the familiar food bowl to him with raised arms. He

Plants of whatever type, especially highly colored kinds, attract budgies. To exclude possible injury by poisoning, remove house plants in the room where a budgie will be set free.

will not be able to hold out for long. If he does though, then we try the same thing again approximately every ten minutes. Sooner or later he will fly on the hand and will immediately begin to crack seeds hungrily, oblivious to his surroundings. Then we can carry him back to the cage along with the food bowl, which ends the first liberty.

With time it will go better and better, and the budgie will soon learn to fly back in the cage on his own as soon as he is hungry, so that one can close the door behind him.

A requirement for this, of course, is that the bird is never fed outside the cage, not even with treats. All food must be offered strictly in the cage.

Observant budgies will soon figure out when they are supposed to be locked up again but do not want to be yet. Even when they are right in the act of feeding, they dart out of the cage faster than one can get to the cage and close the door. Then one must resort to trickery: with the aid of a piece of spray millet—as long as he does not constantly have a supply in the cage—or a fresh bunch of chickweed, one lures him right back in the cage. When he is busy with the treat, one quickly closes the door.

The bird should not be allowed to fly around unsupervised. This especially applies when people are eating meals. The always inquisitive budgie would like nothing better than to take part in our meals, in order to taste everything possible. But he has no business at the dinner table, because most spicy or

sweet human foods do not agree with him. A few cake or white bread crumbs, a piece of egg or potato, to be sure, will do him no harm, but when he drags his tail through the gravy and marches over the clean tablecloth with it, then many a housewife will rightly take offense—and guests all the more. Also, it cannot be denied that there is a danger of catching or transmitting illnesses.

If on some occasion the budgerigar absolutely refuses to go back in the cage, then we wait for dusk and note where he has perched for the night. We grab him quickly and firmly with the hand and put him back in the cage. Very few budgies will resent this, all the less so if the light is left on for a while until the bird has quieted down completely.

We acclimate a pair of budgerigars to liberty in exactly the same way, but must be content that they do not fly to us as often and seek out our contact, because, after all, they are occupied with each other. Instead, they compensate by engaging in all sorts of other activities, such as gnawing on the wallpaper or furniture, perhaps with the idea of excavating a nest cavity; pulling apart a bouquet of fresh flowers; or chewing a peephole in the curtains. For this reason, two or more budgies should never be allowed to fly around without supervision.

Watching budgerigars at liberty, however will never be boring. The observation of the variety of activities they engage in is tremendously diverting. If one has discovered something new, the others follow its example; for example, playing with marbles or throwing paper clips from the table. Everything is properly considered, and if one does something, the others will follow every move with cocked heads deep in thought before joining in.

Even a number of budgerigars kept together can be lured back in the cage with treats.

It is not a bad method to first acquire one bird and to tame it enough that it comes to the keeper voluntarily, moves surely in the room, and goes back to the cage on its own when it is hungry. Only then is a second bird or several more purchased. The new birds will immediately start to imitate everything the established bird does, and will soon venture to come to people without the need for lengthy taming efforts, particu-

Acclimating

Like a magnet, mirrors attract budgies. This lutino budgie is visibly enjoying its own reflection.

larly after they see that nothing happens to the already tame budgie, but on the contrary that it even gets scratched.

It is unnecessary to let a flock of budgies kept in a flight cage or, better yet, in an indoor aviary, out of their cage, all the less if their home is large enough to permit them to fly. For this reason, one should not install too many perches, only enough so that the birds can roost in the upper third of the flight cage (which healthy birds always prefer) without being crowded, and so that they can comfortably reach food and water. It is also worthwhile to equip indoor aviaries with natural branches instead of buying hardwood perches, because they can easily be replaced as soon as they are gnawed away. The gnawing on natural branches, for which all nonpoisonous deciduous woods are suited (preferably willow or fruit tree, but also beech, birch, or hazelnut), is moreover a welcome and natural occupational therapy, and through the intake of tree sap is also a source of vitamins and trace elements.

Teaching the bird to talk

Once the young budgie has become so trusting that it has become steady and confiding, and, above all, also likes to perch on the hand, we can begin teaching it to talk. The morning or evening hours are best for this purpose, because the birds are the most alert at these times. We say a few simple words to the pupil, always in the same rhythm and the same pitch. It is important for the first words in particular as well as the name chosen for the bird to contain more vowels than consonants, because vowels are easier for the bird to imitate than consonants.

The first few words or a short sentence must now be constantly repeated until the budgie starts to mimic them. There is no point in introducing new words or sentences before the first have been learned and the bird repeats them clearly— also spontaneously without having them spoken in front of it. This takes—depending on the aptitude of both the teacher and student—weeks or even months. Up until an age of six months a budgerigar can still learn to talk, but sometimes the bird suddenly starts after one has long since written off its talent.

There is little point in continuing the instruction for hours on end. The lesson should only last as long as budgie listens attentively and at the same time perches steadily on the finger and possibly blinks his eyes. If he starts to groom or even flies away, then it is better to end the instruction until the next suitable opportunity.

Only when the first short sentence has been properly learned should one begin with a new one. Once this first hurdle has been cleared with a budgie, he usually learns new things surprisingly fast, and occasionally combines what he has learned in a comical way, sometimes such that it almost seems to make sense. A talented bird will also soon learn expressions that he hears repeatedly in his environment, without having been taught them on purpose; for example, good day, goodbye, Hello, and names it often hears on the telephone. Unfortunately he can also learn things that are unfit for good company, so that one should exercise some caution when using these expressions in the bird's presence!

A budgie at liberty can be approached quietly and a finger offered to it. Wait patiently for it to stand on both feet on the finger and lift the budgie slowly up and down, avoiding jerky motions.

Nevertheless, one should never make the mistake of wanting to anthropomorphize an animal—whatever kind it might be. A talking parrot can never understand the meaning of a sentence, no matter how well it can say it; only occasionally will it associate specific words with the appropriate situation, and then only because it heard them exclusively in that situation. This can be shown in certain comical absurdities that are combined, such as, Give me a kiss, shame on budgie, don't do that. Counting may be produced in the correct sequence, but is just as likely to be reversed (although Muller-Bierl claims that scientific tests have shown that budgerigars can understand the numbers one to six).

It is very practical from the start to teach the bird not only its name, but also its address, because many a bird that escaped and landed on another family's windowsill was returned only for this reason.

Speaking as clearly as possible is especially important. Many talking budgerigars mumble in a manner that only their owner understands. It is always somewhat embarrassing when such a bird is proudly presented and one understands practically nothing. Budgerigars in any case have a tendency to interweave words and entire sentences with their chattering natural song and to recite a whole potpourri of this kind. For this reason, the bird must be able to mimic speech very clearly if it is

It is certainly gratifying to have a pet budgie perch upon your shoulder on command. It is worth the time you spent in the training of your pet. It will be twice as pleasant if the budgie can talk, also.

to be understood by strangers, which is all the more reason that the words should be repeated slowly and clearly for the bird, and not in too low a pitch. The little bird itself will supply the faster rhythm later, because this is consistent with its natural twittering.

For budgie fanciers with very little time, today there are also recorded tapes with suitable simple words that can be played for the bird at opportune moments. Americans who run professional talking schools for parrots are supposed to have had good success with this method. It verges on animal cruelty, however, to force the bird to listen to such recordings constantly, not to mention that the personal contact is lacking, which is so important for the well-being and lasting confidence of a singly kept budgerigar. Despite all efforts, not every bird, whether male or female, can learn to mimic human speech. Intelligence, so far as it should be discussed in this regard, differs just as much from individual to individual as with other living creatures—human beings included. On the other hand, budgies with no talent for talking can be just as lovable and devoted as great talking artists. It has nothing to do with the color or breed, and it is mistaken to assume that members of the large English show breed are more intelligent simply because they have bigger heads. They are merely easier to tame under certain circumstances, because by nature they have a steady temperament, but, on the other hand, have a tendency to become obese when kept singly.

Happily, some budgerigars that are less talented talkers learn by themselves, to the joy of their owner, to mimic all sorts of sounds, like coughing, throat clearing, laughing, sneezing, squeaking doors, the wolf whistle, or a short, often whistled tune. They also learn to imitate the calls of other birds; the chirping of House Sparrows is especially easy for them because it is quite similar to their own attraction calls, but they also learn portions of proper bird songs. In declamatory moods they again recite a potpourri from this, which can be exceptionally entertaining.

Finally, it is also possible for an older talking budgerigar to be a teacher for a younger one. Nevertheless, some luck is needed for this.

This young man is coaxing his pet to pick a seed held in his mouth. Thus the budgie appears to be in the act of "kissing" as it reaches for the seed.

One should not give up on trying to teach the bird to talk until the end of the first year of life, because one also finds slow learners that only begin to mimic after they reach sexual maturity. What they have heard for months on end without showing a reaction may be impressed in their memory, and may return.

BEHAVIOR

Budgerigars are distinctly social birds which spend their entire lives, whether in the breeding range or on migration, in the company of others of their own kind. For this reason, a single bird needs contact just as much and will only suffer if it is isolated for a fairly long time. The penetrating contact calls, which can be heard over a considerable distance, that it gives in such situations in the wild serve to reunite a straggler with the flock. In the cage, which it cannot escape from, these calls are often accompanied by nervous wingbeats.

This is also the explanation for the following instinct that is expressed when the provider leaves the room in which the tame budgerigar is at liberty. Accidents unfortunately easily result through carelessness, when a door is closed in front of the rapidly approaching bird or it is even caught in the doorframe. Some birds like to patter behind unnoticed on foot and are consequently easily stepped on. Such—usually fatal—accidents are particularly sad, because they are the result of the budgie's attachment to its owner. They do not occur with birds kept in pairs, because the following instinct then is principally directed toward the other bird, and a pair following the keeper is more easily noticed.

Gnawing

The inclination of most parrots—including budgerigars—to gnaw on wood is not a bad habit or vandalism, but on the contrary is connected with their feeding and nest building habits. In the wild, the bark and juicy pith of various trees are part of the diet. For this reason the furniture is also gnawed on, because there could naturally be something better underneath. And if not, it is after all still fun to watch the falling shavings, particularly if one is bored.

Females in the wild form a suitable nest cavity out of holes in tree branches by gnawing, and sometimes attempt to

Behavior

Preoccupation with each other is normal behavior for budgies. Togetherness is expected, as they eat as a group and fly in a flock in the wild.

do this instinctively even if they are not in breeding condition. For this reason females are at times worse, or at least more persistent, wood destroyers than males, and it is better not to leave them unsupervised in a room at liberty. By scolding and carefully shooing them away from the spot they have chosen for gnawing, they can easily be dissuaded from this activity, because they quickly learn what the little woman doesn't like. This, of course, does not mean that they will not try it again if left alone!

Bare from boredom

Boredom is usually the cause of the onerous and disfiguring feather plucking of many parrots and budgies, particularly singly kept birds. Unfortunately, it can easily become a permanent habit when birds accidentally discover that plucked, still growing feathers (that is, feathers that are still sheathed and filled with blood) taste good when these sheaths are drawn through the bill. Some budgies do this even in the middle of the molt, when many blood-filled sheaths are present. They do it even though plucking out the sheaths is apparently painful and

A dramatic demonstration of the extent of the wing span of a normal budgie with a full complement of wing feathers, unclipped.

they sometimes even screech at the same time. The owner could then easily be led to believe that the bird is either deathly ill or that it has lost its mind. Illness is seldom the cause, even if some experts believe that feather plucking could also be triggered by a deficiency of an active agent; for example, of certain minerals. Supplements containing a full assortment of minerals (of which most are present in a varied diet anyway) help only in rare cases, above all when feather plucking has only just become a fixed habit.

Feather pluckers are anything but a pretty sight. Only the plumage that the bird cannot reach with its bill—on the head, nape, and mantle, as well as the wings and tail, whose sturdy feathers the bird cannot manage—is still present. The rest of the body is bare, only covered with sparse down, or even bitten to a bloody mess. All newly sprouting feathers are immediately bitten off again or are torn out. The bird can no longer fly and is highly susceptible to colds.

One should never let it get to this stage; instead, one should try something against it at the first sign of feather plucking. The pet bird field has produced various products that remedy the common problem of feather plucking. The bitter substance contained in the formula immediately deters the act of feather plucking, which is a destructive activity. In addition there are some household remedies which normally are used to curtail the thumb sucking habits of children but are successful and help in the same way, but they are less effective than the specialized bird products.

It can also easily happen that an apparently cured budgie will start plucking feathers again one day, so that a renewed treatment will be necessary.

The exposed wing feathers of this budgie are naturally short, not clipped. This genetic abnormality is called "French Moult." It is not fatal or contagious, but this budgerigar should not be bred.

Alarm!

All budgerigars, both tame birds and those used for breeding, occasionally have a tendency to be wild in the cage during the night, often for no apparent reason, and at times even screech fearfully. When this happens with house pets, one should then turn on the light immediately and talk reassuringly to the birds. Nevertheless, it sometimes takes a long time until they finally calm down and return to their roosting places. The light must not be turned off beforehand, because otherwise they will become wild again.

With cage birds, this behavior does not have any negative consequences, other than that they will be a little tired the next day, but budgerigars that are kept in fairly large aviaries, in which they fly with force against wire mesh and windows, unfortunately often suffer serious injuries—up to broken necks that result in death. For this reason, most breeders have turned to the practice of installing night-lights, which use little electricity and illuminate the space enough that the birds fluttering around can see obstacles in time and that incubating females which have fallen out of their nest boxes can find their way back before the eggs or small young get cold.

This foolish behavior might seem puzzling to the reader who is unfamiliar with animal behavior, but there are clearly understandable reasons for it if one knows more about the life of the little Australian in the wild.

Like all creatures in the wild, budgerigars are exposed to various dangers, whereby hawks and owls as birds-of-prey are their principal enemies. If a flock of budgerigars is feeding on the ground in the daytime, a few sentries always stay behind in nearby trees or other elevated places in order to sound the alarm at the slightest hostile approach. The birds scatter in all directions and only come together again by means of their contact calls, which can be heard over a considerable distance, when the danger has passed. The same thing happens in the

To keep a newly acquired budgerigar calm at night, keep the cage away from house traffic, perhaps suspended from a hook in the ceiling (not shown) of a quiet room.

Behavior

An aviary is usually built on the side of the house away from the street, to avoid the noise and pollution from passing motor vehicles. Some type of lighting is recommended to allow the birds to perceive their surroundings at night.

hot time of day during the midday rest and in the night, because budgerigars are light sleepers and react to the slightest strange noise. The first bird to hear a strange noise gives an alarm call, and all of the birds scatter immediately. In the virtually treeless plains they can scarcely injure themselves even in the dark, and it never gets so dark there that they cannot see obstacles like trees, bushes, and hills in time to avoid them.

It is different in a cage in a dark room or in an aviary, however large it might be. The wire or wood walls always set relatively confined limits, which do not exist in the wild.

Menacing sounds, such as cats creeping by or approaching owls, automobile headlights in conjuction with engine sounds, approaching footsteps, or even any strange noise, no matter how slight, could trigger an alarm—could, but does not necessarily have to. There is no reason to tiptoe around where the budgerigar or budgerigars are sleeping. The alarm can also be triggered by any sort of air disturbance that we cannot even detect. It occurs unexpectedly from time to time, whereby it is interesting to note that this instinct of species preservation has been maintained in budgerigars bred under human care over many generations.

BREEDING BUDGIES

In the wild, budgies are cavity nesters, breeding in eucalyptus and dead tree stumps with porous wood and many holes. The female shaves the hole into a suitable shape with her sharp bill, and the shavings create the nesting material. In their native Australia, budgies breed in the spring months of December to February. Usually they are colony breeders, making the chances of a lone pair starting a family pretty slim. Budgies seem to need the competitiveness of the group situation to become interested in reproduction.

There are cases when a lone hen or two hens will heed the urge of nature and produce eggs (which are always infertile). If this should happen, leave two of the eggs with your hen to satisfy her maternal instinct (removing them in a couple of weeks). Of course, in order to get fertile eggs, it is necessary to have two birds of the opposite sex. The sex of a mature budgie is easily determined. Adult birds have waxy skin around their nostrils, called the cere, which is a rich blue color in males and whitish, brown, or tan in the female.

As stimulation from companions is lacking for birds kept in captivity, the single pair if not given a nest box does not usually breed, though they will stick closely together, billing and cooing. When properly conditioned, provided with a nest box, and so inclined, the cock courts the hen. He will bow many times before the female and finally feed her from his crop. The actual mating is preceded and accompanied by a great deal of billing and mutual preening. Her cere turns dark brown and appears wrinkled. His cere is plump and bright blue; his eyes sparkle and the pupils expand and contract rapidly.

The mating act is accomplished by the male's mounting the female; balancing himself on her with fluttering wings, he swings his tail under hers and the sperm is transferred. Unless this takes place, the eggs when laid will be infertile.

A typical clutch of budgerigar eggs. The relative size of the eggs can be judged by comparing them to the size of the hand.

Egglaying starts about eight days after mating, with one laid every other day. The maximum number of eggs for a budgie is nine, but it is best to leave only four or five in the nest so the parents aren't overtaxed caring for too many young. The hen will remain constantly in the nest box (being kindly fed by the cock) after the first egg is laid, so the first clutch of eggs will be hatched in about 18 days. The chicks hatch about two days apart. The chick will cut its way out of the egg using a little thornlike pin (eggtooth) on its beak. This is followed by strong shoulder movements which lift the sawed-through section of the shell. After that the young nestling takes its first few breaths of air and then rests after this enormous physical effort. During that time the lower portion of the new chick, still inside the egg's shell, dries out and the remainder of the shell detaches itself automatically. Only then will the hen help by removing the empty shells from the nest.

If the budgie baby is alive and well, one can hear its voice by the seventeenth incubation day inside the egg. It is a continuous drawn-out chirping sound, which—after hatching—is quite penetrating. This sound is the signal for the female to feed this youngster for the first time. It is almost a little miracle that the female, even in the darkness of the nest box, cares for

Two hatchlings struggling to move between two still unhatched eggs.

her chicks of different sizes and ages individually, and not even the youngest fledgling will be forgotten. A hatchling chick is smaller than the foot of its l5-day-old brother or sister, but it will be as well fed as the others. Most budgies are very good parents. Many males will help feed the young right from the start. In fact, many will even attempt to help with the incubating, as long as the female permits it.

The method nature employs to feed baby budgies is very interesting and unique. The young are fed with a substance regurgitated from the crop called budgie milk. Little is known about this substance, but it is rich in fat and protein. The mother feeds her newly hatched babies about four times an hour. The intervals are longer as the young grow, with the father taking a more active role in feeding as they get older.

Excuse me, but budgie babies are very homely. The parents keep them covered and warm. They are born almost naked and blind. In a few days the eyes open and the down appears. It takes two weeks until the regular color plumage appears from underneath the thick down. At the age of three weeks the nestlings begin to look more like budgerigars. At that time the wing and tail feathers break out of their stalks, and the original, somewhat spiny appearance due to the feather stalks begins to be replaced with the shiny and smooth budgie plumage. In two weeks the nestling can raise its head and move

Breeding Budgies

about. The babies are completely feathered at about five weeks, and it is then they first venture out of the nest box. This imminent event can be recognized by a peculiar sound through the nest box walls. It resembles the humming of tiny airplane propellors...the young are exercising their wings.

The exact age when young birds will fly from the nest box, while variable, is usually between five and six weeks. Healthy birds can fly quite well as soon as they leave their boxes (but landing takes practice). In a few days they will fly about just as well as their parents. They are dependent on their father for another week or ten days for food, and it is he who will coax the young to the seed source. When the last chick in the nest has been flying for about a week, it is safe to remove all the young from the parents and put them in a cage by themselves.

When the babies are no longer being fed by their parents, it is a good idea to crack their seed with a rolling pin for the first few days and place it in a shallow saucer on the floor of the cage, since they may not have sense enough to find it in the seed cup.

The adult female pays no attention once her brood has left. In fact, freshly laid eggs appear in the nest again even before the last nestling has gone. This can cause some problems—maybe you don't want to go through this again. If you don't want more eggs, remove the nesting box.

Budgerigar nestlings at various stages of development. In time the spiky appearance of the plumage will disappear when the feathers start to unroll.

The old proverb an ounce of prevention is better than a pound of cure applies especially to budgerigars. If no gross errors in feeding and care are made, serious illnesses need scarcely to be reckoned with in the first four years of life with this robust species of bird. Males are capable of reproduction for six to at most eight years, and females for four to at most five years. Whether birds are used for breeding or not, the time of the change of life between the fifth and eighth years is critical for both sexes, in which many die from some illness or other. This is comparable to a human age of 50 to 70, which is why one should try to consider it as objectively as possible. In fact, budgerigars can attain a maximum age of 15 to even 18 years, but this is just as exceptional as our hundred-year-olds.

ILLNESSES

If a budgie has survived the critical time up to the eighth year of life without ever having been seriously ill, then one can count on it enjoying a few more years of life. Senility often sets in, but only shortly before death. In one instance an eleven-year-old continued to talk clearly and frequently even though it could barely still hold onto a perch with its gouty feet.

A budgerigar that—for whatever reason—does not feel well sleeps more than usual and at the same time perches on both legs, whereas a healthy adult bird always sleeps on one leg and the other one is drawn into the belly plumage.

Once again, the best way to prevent illness is to feed your budgie a nutritious, well balanced diet and to keep your pet's equipment and surroundings clean and germ-free—and of course parasite-free as well. If you have reason to believe that your budgie is under the weather and the condition persists without your being able to pin down the source of the trouble, perhaps your best course of action is to contact your veterinarian for professional advice.

The following books by T.F.H. Publications are available at pet shops everywhere.

ENCYCLOPEDIA OF BUDGERIGARS By Georg A. Radtke (H-1027)

In this most comprehensive of this well-known author's works on budgerigars, the initial chapters present an overview of budgerigars in the wild and in captivity, treat the various aspects of a complete budgerigar diet in detail, and then discuss breeding strategies and the prevention and treatment of disease. *Illustrated with 148 color and 44 black-and-white photos. Hard cover, 5½ x 8", 320 pp.*

SUGGESTED READING

BUDGERIGAR HANDBOOK
By Ernest H. Hart (H-901)

Offers complete coverage of every subject of importance to the budgerigar enthusiast. Included are discussions of modes of inheritance, basic breeding techniques, aviaries and equipment, feeding and management, shows and the Standard, matings and color expectations, and training the pet budgerigar. Color varieties are shown in photographs. *Illustrated with 104 color and 57 black-and-white photos. Hard cover, 5½ x 8", 251 pp.*

STARTING RIGHT WITH BUDGERIGARS by Risa Teitler (PS-793)

Written to provide reliable, easy-to-understand information to new owners of budgerigars. The author is a noted bird trainer who draws on her special expertise in explaining just what to do when caring for, feeding, and handling a pet parakeet. *Illustrated with 67 color and 11 black-and-white photos. Hard cover, 8f½ x 11", 80 pp.*

Index